# Crochet Guide for Beginners:

Discovering the Art of Handmade Creations with Essential Techniques, Timeless Patterns, and Beginner-Friendly Tutorials

## By:

## Roan Kendrick

# Table of Contents

# Introduction

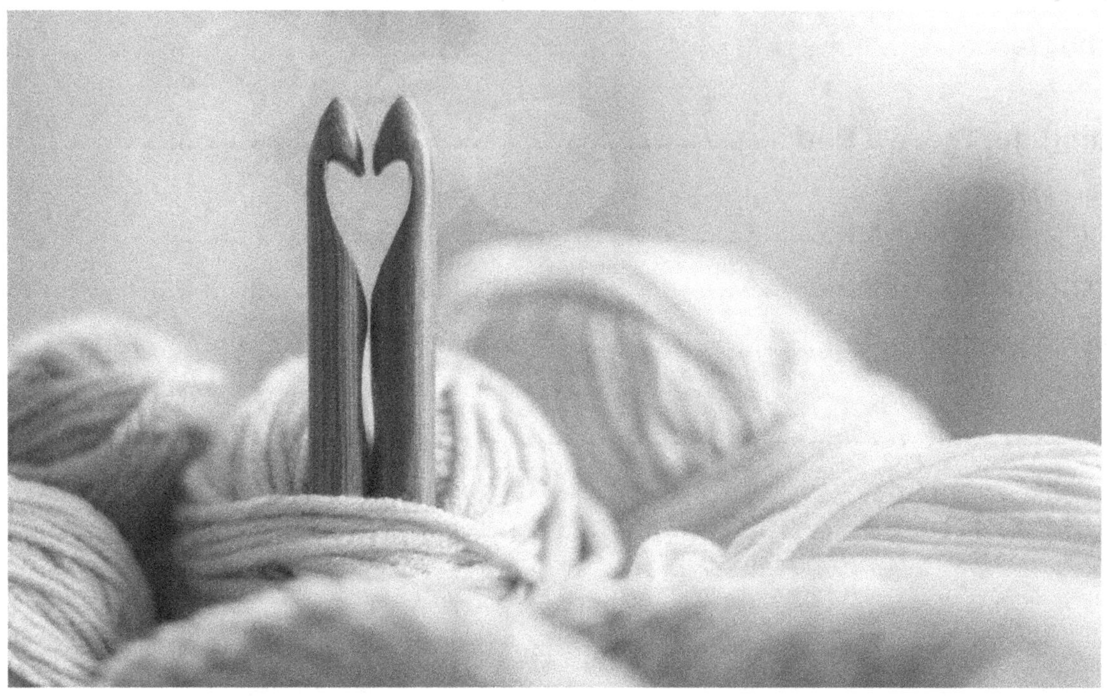

Crochet, I hear, is a truly fascinating hobby. It has a mysterious past that nobody really knows much about. There are claims that it was first developed in Arabia and subsequently transferred to Spain via trade routes, while some assert that it originated in Europe or South America. It's like a mystery novel but with knitting instead of crime.

Crochet's popularity skyrocketed across Europe in the nineteenth century. People were producing anything from doilies and tablecloths to clothes after the publication of pattern books. Fast forward to the present day, and you can find crochet used in cutting-edge ways by artists in sculptures and installations. It's not something only grandmother does for fun anymore!

Several variations of crochet have been adopted by various cultures. It was a means of supplementary income for people in Ireland. Irish lace, have you heard of it? Definitely crocheting there. One style of crocheted bag found in South America is the Mochila. Among the Wayuu people of Colombia, it is a long-standing custom.

Crochet is a worldwide amalgam of history, culture, and art, not just a craft using yarn and hooks. That's awesome, right?

Crocheting has several benefits for your health, including creating adorable hats and warm blankets. Let's start by discussing stress reduction. You know how you feel so relaxed when you're in the "zone"? That's what crocheting does. It resembles a type of meditation in that when you pay attention to your stitches and patterns, the turmoil of the outside world simply vanishes. It really is healing in every way.

The possibilities are now endless in terms of creativity. Create patterns, experiment with colors, and even create three-dimensional shapes. Painting with yarn, but better! There are always projects to work on, and there's nothing like the satisfaction of finishing one. Priceless.

Crocheting is useful in a practical sense as well. Looking for a last-minute gift? Knit a scarf. Want to modernize the style of your house? Create stylish cushion covers. Even better, you can sell your work to get some extra money.

Hey, remember motor skills as well. Manipulating the hook and yarn can enhance your dexterity and hand-eye coordination. It resembles a finger workout, but it's far more enjoyable.

Therefore, crocheting is a great way to unwind, stimulate creativity, or create something beautiful.

You're interested in improving your crochet skills. Awesome! Let's dissect it.

We started with the "Beginners." These people are just starting and learning the basic crochet stitches, such as single, double, and slip ones. If you're here, you're making simple items like dishcloths or even a straightforward scarf. We all have to start somewhere, so don't worry!

You will then reach the "Intermediate" level. You're now getting to the good part, which includes more intricate patterns, color variations, and fundamental shaping. Consider granny squares, caps, and even straightforward clothing. You've gotten into the crochet rhythm, so you're no longer a rookie!

The "Advanced" level follows. Ah, the Jedi Masters of crochet! You will need to work with complex patterns, multicolored projects, and precise sculpting. Now, you're making intricately stitched garments, intricate afghans, and items like lace. Now, your hook resembles a magic wand.

However, there's still more! Even the "Expert" area is explored by some. Full-fledged works of art, three-dimensional shapes, and crocheted items that most people find hard to believe are all included. "Did you really make that?" is the question.

Therefore, there is always something new to learn and aspire to, no matter where you are in your crochet journey. The possibilities are endless, from learning the fundamentals to producing a masterpiece in crochet!

You obviously want to know what noteworthy projects and strategies are covered in the book. You're in for a treat, I assure you.

First up is this incredibly stylish "Tapestry Crochet Tote Bag." We're delving into the tapestry crochet method, which enables you to make interesting color patterns without cutting your yarn. Yes, with this fashionable bag, you'll be the talk of the town.

Prepare yourself now for the "Ombré Throw Blanket." You'll learn how to do ombré, the cool color gradient you see everywhere, in crochet. Just picture yourself curled up beneath a blanket that resembles a sunset. Dreamy, no?

Oh, and there's a "Boho Crop Top" that is just exquisite for those of you who are fashionistas. You'll learn how to shape your clothing such that it fits like a glove, as well as basic lace methods. Yes, definitely Instagram-worthy.

Ever heard of "Amigurumi" before? It is a Japanese craft in which miniature stuffed animals are knitted or crocheted. We have a chapter on creating an absurdly adorable "Amigurumi Unicorn." You'll be shaping and building like an expert; it's not simply about fundamental stitches.

There is something for everyone, regardless of your experience with hooking. Get ready to greatly broaden your crochet horizons!

Seriously, this book will become your new best friend. There is something for everyone, from complete beginners to seasoned veterans. I'll give you the skinny.

The first section of "The Supply Spectrum" walks you through all the necessary tools. We are discussing hooks, stitch markers, and other such things.

The sections "All About Yarn" and "Yarn Weight Guidelines" are where you should start if you want to master yarn. Discover how to choose the ideal yarn for any project, from fingering weight to chunky.

Your cheat sheets will be "Crochet Cornerstones" and "The Crocheter's Dictionary." We have you prepared for everything from knowing acronyms to translating crochet jargon.

Prepared to unravel patterns? "A Guide to Pattern Reading" decodes all those confusing crochet patterns like your own Rosetta Stone.

The "Stitch Mastery" section is where you'll go into the fundamentals. Learn the basic stitches first, then use the "Advanced Stitches" to up your game.

Additionally, we provide information for you on "Techniques for Shaping and Joining," "Colorwork and Patterns," and "Special Techniques." You'll be mastering yarn manipulation, making incredible forms, and adding colorful accents like never before.

Then get ready for "Blueprints in Yarn," where we feature crafts like Amigurumi Toys and Granny Square Blankets. Every project, from simple things like potholders to eye-catching things like lace shawls, will help you put everything you've learned into practice.

In addition, "Stitching the Story's End" shows you how to add those final touches that turn a creation into something truly remarkable. It also covers edging techniques and putting parts together.

So, certainly, you have everything you need in this book to advance your crocheting skills. Less talking and Let's start fishing!

# The Supply Spectrum

## What you'll need

### Basic Essentials

You're about to start a really exciting journey. But first, let's speak about the fundamentals because you'll need a few things to get things going in the correct direction.

Hooks are the tools that transform yarn into warm scarves, adorable stuffed animals, and other cool things. Each hook size corresponds to a certain yarn weight; more on yarn shortly. Hooks are available in a variety of sizes. As a beginner, get a hook set with diameters ranging from 4mm to 6mm. These are the most typical sizes and are excellent for new users.

Let's talk about yarn now. There are countless varieties, but to start out easy, use a basic yarn like acrylic or cotton. Acrylic is quite flexible and excellent for practicing. A fantastic option is cotton, especially for tasks like making dishcloths. For your initial projects, stick to worsted-weight or medium-weight yarn. It is manageable and functions admirably with the 4-6mm hooks we described.

**Stitch Markers:** When working on a project, these tiny men act as the Hansel and Gretel tale's breadcrumbs, guiding you in the right direction. When you first start, remember where you should start each round or which precise stitch needs to be increased or decreased. Stitch markers can help with it. Simply insert one into the stitch, serving as a bookmark for your crochet project. They can be simple plastic ones.

**Yarn Needle:** You've completed your craft; congrats (high five! ), but now you have many yarn ends hanging around. I present the yarn needle. These blunt needles feature a big eye that makes it simple to thread yarn through them. You'll use it to weave the ends and finish your job neatly and efficiently.

That's all there is to it! You don't need more than these supplies to begin your crocheting journey: hooks, yarn, stitch markers, and a needle. Prepare yourself to connect your way to some incredible inventions!

**Intermediate Additions**

So you've got the fundamentals down, right? Are you prepared to take your crocheting adventure to the next level? Buckle up because we're about to get into the really fantastic stuff that will improve your crafting skills. We're glad you're here, Intermediate Additions!

**Ergonomic Hooks:** Do you recall when you first started learning to ride a bike with training wheels before moving on to a two-wheeler? The crochet equivalent of mountain bikes would be ergonomic hooks. The ergonomic grips on these hooks let you crochet for extended periods without suffering from hand or style cramps. If you intend to work on larger or more intricate tasks, your hands will appreciate this improvement.

**A Variety of Yarns:** You're now prepared to explore the huge and stunning world of yarn! How about some bamboo or alpaca now that you've had your basic acrylic and cotton fill? These yarns provide your work a variety of textures and properties. Are you feeling fancy? Try some cashmere or silk yarn. Additionally, you should experiment with various yarn weights, including lace for delicate shawls, bulky for plush blankets, and everything in between.

**Blocking Boards:** You've probably observed that not all projects turn out perfectly after they're finished. Blocking boards are useful for giving them a little "spa treatment" when necessary. You can use these boards to wet or steam your finished pieces to give them the ideal shape. Do you have a lacy shawl in need of some wingspan? Your first choice is a blocking board. It serves as the equivalent of your crochet projects' finishing school.

**Bonus Tools:** To keep everything organized, look at other devices like yarn winders, row counters, or even a special crochet project bag. These are more like the whipped cream and cherry on top of your crochet sundae than necessary.

There you have it, then. These resources will support you as you take a confident step into intermediate terrain, allowing you to take on more challenging projects and hone your abilities.

**Advanced Arsenal**

As a result, you have advanced to the crochet elite level. You have the talent, style, and creativity to create amazing projects. Let's discuss how some specific tools and materials might further help you develop your advanced skills. You're now in your sophisticated arsenal.

**Specialty Hooks:** You've outgrown standard hooks, so it's time to investigate some unusual designs. Do you know what Tunisian crochet hooks are? These combine the functions of crochet hooks with knitting needles. You can handle several loops at once because they are longer and have a stopper at the end. This makes novel stitches and patterns that couldn't be done with standard hooks possible. It's similar to finding a secret video game level!

You're probably familiar with the fundamentals like wool and cotton, but what about mohair, silk, or even hand-dyed artisan yarns? These finer yarns are ideal for elaborate patterns where each stitch may be a piece of beauty. Fine yarns enhance your efforts to heritage quality, whether a sumptuous silk shawl or an intricately patterned wrap.

You've progressed past basic row counting. Therefore, you need an advanced stitch counter. Advanced stitch counters can maintain track of numerous row patterns, notify you when tasks need to be completed, and even keep track of the locations where stitches should be added or subtracted. To make managing complicated tasks easier, some even sync with mobile apps. Without the small conversation, it's like having a personal crochet assistant!

**Specialized Tools:** This is where the fun stuff comes in, like tangle-free yarn bowls, clip-on stitch markers for elaborate pattern work, and even magnifying lamps for working with fine or small, detailed stitches. Have you ever used a crocheted chart holder? Your crochet adventure will go more smoothly if your pattern is kept front and center so you can read it while working.

# All about Yarn

## Yarn 101

Welcome to Yarn 101, a comprehensive introduction to the warm, vibrant world of yarns. Knowing your yarn is like knowing your components before you prepare a wonderful cuisine. How about we unravel this ball of yarn?

**Cotton:** The timeless! Cotton yarn is comfortable and breathable; it is essentially the jeans and t-shirt of the yarn world. It works well for household items like dishcloths, tablecloths and summer clothing like tanks and t-shirts. It can typically be machine washed, but always check the label to be sure. Just be aware that cotton tends to be heavier and less stretchable.

**Wool:** The original natural material, wool is cozy and stretchy, making it ideal for winter clothing like scarves, blankets, and sweaters. There are several sorts of wool as well, such as the very soft Merino. Wool is difficult to maintain because it frequently needs to be hand-washed and flat-dried to prevent shrinking and felting.

The most often used yarn is acrylic! Acrylic is synthetic, incredibly adaptable, and inexpensive. From beanies to blankets, it works well. Additionally, it may typically be dried and machine-washed. But hey, it's a workhorse that gets the job done. On the other hand, it's not as breathable as natural fibers.

**Blends:** These are hybrid materials, such as cotton linen or a wool-acrylic mix. They combine qualities like the coziness of wool and the toughness of acrylic to give you the best of both worlds. However, blends might be a little tough to take care of, so always check the labels.

**Properties and Applications:** Each yarn has its own "personality." Wool is warm and stretchy, cotton is cold but inelastic, and acrylic is strong but less permeable. Make a judicious choice of yarn for your project, whether a warm winter afghan or a summer shawl.

**Care Instructions:** Always check the care label on the yarn. Some require hand-washing, others can withstand a washing machine, and some need air drying.

There you have it, a quick tour to Yarnville. This information lets you choose the ideal yarn for your upcoming masterpiece.

**Color and Texture**

Are you prepared to add some extra flair to your projects? Let's explore the varied world of crochet's color and texture. They can completely change your creation, so trust me when I say they're like the spices in a recipe.

**Hue selection:** Choosing the perfect hue is more than simply what looks good; it's also about creating the right mood. Softer, milder colors provide a calming effect, while bright, assertive colors can add energy to your work. Consider your project's intended use: Are you making a colorful baby blanket or a chic throw for your couch? Using color can create an atmosphere, communicate a message, or even help your stitches tell a story.

**Methods for Dyeing Yarn:** The manner a yarn is colored can have a significant impact on your project. There are "variegated" yarns, which have many colors throughout the strand, and "solid colors," which are a single, uniform hue. The shades of "Ombre" yarn gradually change. Each dying technique has a distinctive twist that allows you to produce patterns and effects effortlessly. Just consider how magical it would be if a shawl made of ombre yarn automatically changed from light to dark.

Remember to value the importance of texture! The textural vibes of various yarns vary. Chenille yarn is luxuriously smooth, whereas bouclé yarn includes tiny loops that give it a rough, 3D feel. Even your choice of stitch can provide texture. Have you ever used the popcorn stitch to create an elevated, bobbly effect? Creating a tactile experience is key to transforming your project from "Oh, cool" to "OMG, how did you make this?"

When texture and color meet, they can create a powerful combination. For a bold, contemporary aesthetic, picture a tight stitch being worked with a thick, bright red yarn. Or how about a gentle, romantic feel with a pastel, fluffy yarn worked in a lace pattern? There are countless options.

**Accessorizing the Process**

You obviously have your yarn and hooks under control, but what about those little flourishes that can really set your products apart? In fact, it's like picking the ideal jewelry to go with your beautiful ensemble, so let's speak about accessorizing the process!

**Beads:** Picture the sprinkles on a cupcake as beads. They tuck in that additional touch. Beads can add texture and sparkle to everything, from constructing boho-chic bracelets to bringing up a blanket. You can slide them in as you go or string them onto your yarn before you begin. To avoid becoming trapped, ensure your hook is small enough to fit through the bead hole.

**Buttons:** Buttons can be used merely for decoration and fastening. Consider a set of sweet wooden buttons down a baby frock's back or a set of quirky, mismatched buttons bringing life to a simple cardigan. Think of convertible scarves or detachable boot cuffs for examples of how buttons can provide functionality.

**Fabric Linings:** Have you ever constructed a crocheted bag that sagged when you filled it with items? Thanks to a fabric lining, it can have structure, toughness, and a splash of unnoticed color. A plush lining can give extra warmth to wearables like mittens or slippers. Even if you are not a skilled sewer, some fabric glue can do wonders.

Remember to value the practicality and style that zippers and closures can add. A zipped pocket can greatly improve the usability of a bag you're creating. Whether for detachable collars or easy-on baby booties, velcro, and snap closures are useful.

Want to give your project some fun movement using tassels and fringe? Fringe and tassels might be the solution. They can be the finishing touch for blanket corners, shawl edges, or even throw pillow corners. Choose yarns that contrast or enhance your primary project for a striking appearance.

Lastly, but certainly not least, who doesn't adore a nice pom-pom? These fluffy balls of bliss are the icing on your crochet sundae since they are ideal for hat toppers, scarf ends, or even as standalone keychains.

## Yarn weight guidelines

**Lace (or Thread):**

Welcome to the world of ultra-fine yarn, where meticulous workmanship combines with delicate beauty. This material is akin to "fine china" of yarns—too beautiful for regular usage yet utterly gorgeous.

**Best For:** These undertakings require very little light for ethereal shawls, delicate doilies, or gossamer clothing that makes you feel like a character from a fairy tale; lace or thread work beautifully. It's not your go-to for things that require a lot of force; instead, it's all about elegance.

Because of the extreme thinness of the yarn, the smallest hook and needle sizes are advised for crocheting and knitting. These sizes range from 1.5 to 2.25 mm. I promise you'll need those smaller tools to handle this delicate yarn with the care it requires.

Lace or thread is located at the featherweight end of the yarn weight hierarchy. It can take longer to build up because it is lighter than fingering or sports weight, but the rewards are worth it!

**Super Fine (or Fingering, Baby):**

The super fine club with extremely fine yarn that is as delicate as morning dew! We're talking about incredibly fine threads barely thicker than lace yet maintaining their exquisite appeal.

**Best For:** This yarn is fantastic for making baby accessories like soft blankets, adorable booties, and tiny hats. But it's not only for kids; it's also fantastic for simple adult projects! Dreamy shawls, cushy socks, and chic tops are all acceptable attire.

You should use knitting needles or crochet hooks with a size between 2.25 and 3.25 mm for knitting and 2.25 to 3.5 mm for crochet. You have more freedom to maneuver than lace because it's little but not microscopic.

**Fine (or Sport, Baby):**

Interested in learning more about fine or sport yarns? This one is like the "middle child" in the family of lightweight yarns; it's still lightweight but has a little more strength than extremely fine.

**Best For:** Keep in mind warm-weather baby clothing like rompers, sweaters, or even light blankets ideal for chilly summer evenings. With this yarn, you may create gorgeous light clothing like flowy cardigans and airy tops.

You'll use a slightly chunkier set of tools—knitting needles measuring 3.25–3.75 mm and crochet hooks measuring 3.5–4.5 mm. Just the correct size for that fine yarn—neither too big nor too small.

**Light (or DK, Light Worsted):**

Light, DK, or worsted weight yarn This is the universally popular, cozy, and comfortable hoodie of the yarn world.

**Best For:** The options are endless! We're talking blankets that are the ideal combination of warm and breathable, comfy sweaters that aren't overly thick, and transitional-weather-appropriate scarves. Additionally, it's awesome for both adult-sized and children's clothing.

You should purchase knitting needles between 3.75 and 4.5 mm and crochet hooks between 4.5 and 5.5 mm. They are precisely the correct size to handle the somewhat thicker texture of this yarn.

So, light/DK yarn has your back if you're looking for the ideal mid-range yarn that is neither too light nor too hefty.

**Medium (or Worsted, Afghan, Aran):**

Meet medium yarn, commonly referred to as worsted, Afghan, or Aran yarn, the MVP of the yarn industry. The Swiss Army Knife of yarn, this thing really can do it all!

**Best For:** Do you want to knit a blanket? Done. Warm sweaters for the winter? You nailed it. What about mittens, scarves, or even stuffed animals? Yes, this yarn literally has you covered. It's the go-to for many projects, so if you want adaptability, it's ideal.

Knitting needles should be between 4.5 and 5.5 mm, while crochet hooks should be between 5.5 and 6.5 mm. They're substantial enough to handle the thickness of the yarn without being overly large to lose detail.

So, medium yarn is like that dependable friend who's always there for you if you're just starting out in knitting or crocheting or even an experienced pro.

**Bulky (or Chunky, Rug):**

The linebacker of yarns is thick, chunky, or rug yarn. Big, brave, and prepared to take on any task that calls for some weight and warmth!

Suitable in Cold? Which cold? This yarn lets you quickly create super-warm caps, fluffy scarves, and cuddly blankets. And rugs, too? Your floors will be wearing a layer that is soft and cuddly.

Size of Needle or Hook Suggestion: Go big or go home, right? You'll need knitting needles in the 5.5-8 mm range and crochet hooks between 6.5 and 9 mm. The perfect size to handle all that mass is these bad boys.

**Super Bulky (or Super Chunky):**

Are you prepared to enter the yarn universe in full Hulk mode? A weightlifter at the gym, super bulky or super chunky yarn, is all about the hard lifting and getting results quickly.

**Best For:** Do you have a free weekend? You could make a complete blanket out of this yarn. The truth. It's also terrible for those ridiculously cozy scarves and headgear that laugh off the winter chill. I promise you'll feel as comfortable as a bug.

It's time to remove the heavy equipment—crochet hooks that are 9 mm and larger knitting needles that begin at 8 mm. The monster trucks of crafting equipment, essentially.

**Jumbo:**

Hold onto your hooks and needles because we'll enter the Jumbo zone! The Godzilla of the crafting world is this yarn. Seriously, it is enormous.

Have you ever tried crocheting on your arm? Yes, that's right—this giant allows you to use your arms instead of needles. We're talking about large blankets that can be made in a maximum of two hours. Additionally, this yarn is a monster for any craft where bigger is unquestionably better.

Prepare yourself; knitting needles start at 12.75 mm, and crochet hooks that are 15 mm or larger. You'll need this equipment, which resembles oars, to handle this enormous yarn.

# Crochet Cornerstones

## The Crocheter's Dictionary

- Chain (ch). Folks, this is the point at which everything starts! The first step in any crochet project is to create a chain.
- The Single Crochet stitch (abbreviated as sc) is the most fundamental. This stitch is ideal for producing solid fabrics because of its short length and high thread density.
- The double crochet stitch (often abbreviated as DC) is a taller version of the single crochet stitch, giving your fabric height and a little more flexibility.
- This stitch, slip stitch or sl st, functions like a period after a crochet sentence. You can use it to join rounds, finish a project, or shift your yarn to a different location without adding height.
- Yarn Over (yo) is a crochet term for looping the yarn around your hook. It's an essential step in the process of making stitches. Flip your work so you are

crocheting down the row in the opposite direction. This step is often performed after a turning chain.

- A gauge is a sample swatch used to determine the size of the stitches and rows in your project so that it does not turn out too big or too little.
- The final act, often known as "Fasten Off" (FO)! This indicates that you will cut the yarn and then secure it so the project can be finished.
- Half Double Crochet (HDC) is a half-step stitch between a single and double crochet. It is considered to be intermediate crochet terminology. It offers a greater height than SC but less than DC does.
- These names refer to the two loops at the top of each stitch and are abbreviated as "FLO" and "BLO." Front Loop Only (FLO) and Back Loop Only (BLO). Creating texture requires either working in one loop or the other. When you need to narrow your piece, you will decrease the stitch count by working two stitches together to produce one. This will bring the total number of stitches down by one.
- The reverse of a decrease, an increase, involves adding an additional stitch to your project to make it wider.
- Cluster Stitch refers to working several unfinished stitches into a single space, which are then completed to form a textured "cluster."
- A chain stitch and a slip stitch are worked into the same thread to make a picot, which is a little loop. Gives the edge a decorative touch.
- Wetting or heating your finished piece to set the stitches and even out any flaws in the blocking process. It is comparable to a spa day for your crocheting!
- Crocheting in a spiral or circular pattern is known as "in-the-round" and is typically used to make amigurumi or caps.
- Rather than stitching them together afterward, you can join motifs or panels as you go with the join-as-you-go (JAYG) technique.
- Stitch Marker. A device for marking a particular stitch or beginning point; frequently used in crafts with intricate patterns or when working in the round.

Terms for Experts:

- The Bullion Stitch is a crochet stitch that looks like a twisted spiral and is similar to the curly fry stitch.
- The term "magic circle" refers to a method of beginning round crochet projects without creating a hole in the project's center.
- This crochet mixes knitting and crochet, typically calling for a hook designed specifically for Tunisian crochet. Produces a material with a higher density.
- The Japanese craft of making amigurumi is cropping various stuffed animals or items in miniature sizes.
- Post Stitch. A type of texture-adding stitch that involves working stitches around the post of another stitch rather than the loops of that stitch.
- Foundation single crochet, often known as FSC, is a crocheting method that combines the creation of a beginning chain and a row of single crochet stitches into a single operation.
- [] or (). These abbreviations denote a set of stitches that must be worked in a certain sequence or more than once. The pattern between the asterisks is almost always a series of stitches that need to be worked more than once.
- Sk means to omit the following stitch.
- Tog. Together, typically used to refer to decreasing stitches; for example, "single crochet two together" (abbreviated as "sc2tog") means "single crochet two stitches together."
- RS and WS stand for the "Right Side" and "Wrong Side" of the project, respectively.
- Rep: Repeat the instructions given in the previous sentence.
- Yo. Knot your yarn. Typically followed by additional directions such as "yo, pull through 2 loops."
- Additional abbreviations include ch-sp, which refers to the space behind a chain where the hook is inserted to make the following stitch.

- A place marker, or PM, is utilized when a stitch or space needs to be designated for later use.
- A multi-color project's main color is referred to as the MC.
- Contrasting Color (CC) refers to a project's secondary color or colors.
- Space(s). Space(s) typically shows where to place the hook for the subsequent stitch.
- The beginning is often known as the beginning of a round or row.
- Half-treble crochet (htr) is frequently used in UK terminology and is marginally taller than half-double crochet.
- To create a textured stitch known as a "bobble," numerous taller stitches—typically double or treble crochet—must be partially completed in the same stitch or space before being joined at the top.
- Popcorn. A bobble-like object created by working individual stitches, pulling the hook, then re-inserting it from the front to bring the first and last stitches together to create a "popcorn."
- A series of stitches—typically double crochets—worked into the same area or stitch to produce a fan-like form is known as a shell.

## A Guide to Pattern Reading

You've finally gotten the hang of the fundamental stitches, and now you're staring at a crochet pattern that looks like some kind of cryptic equation. Don't be concerned! The process of deciphering crochet patterns is analogous to progressing through levels in a video game. Believe me, it's a skill you'll be glad to have. Let's not waste any time and get into the enchanted world of pattern reading.

### The Elements That Comprise a Crochet Pattern Title and Designer

 In most cases, the pattern will begin with the title of the project as well as the name of the designer. At this point, you should give a fist bump to the creative mastermind behind the design.

Three different skill levels are available: beginner, intermediate, and advanced. This provides you with an indication of whether the pattern will be an easy stroll or a challenging ascent of Mount Everest.

The following is a list of the materials you will need, including the type and quantity of yarn, the size of the hook, and any other materials you may require, such as buttons, stitch markers, or stuffing.

**Indicator:** You must take advantage of this! Using a gauge swatch, you can determine whether your stitches are too tight or too loose for the project. If you choose to disregard it, you might find yourself with a baby blanket that is large enough to be used as a handkerchief.

A guide to the pattern's abbreviations, or shorthand, is used. The term "double crochet" is shortened to "dc," the word "skip" is changed to "sk," and so on.

Pattern Notes are supplemental information and helpful pointers the designer provides to assist you in completing the project.

**The Actual Pattern:** At long last, we've arrived at the juicy part of the project! Depending on what it is that you're creating, this is typically broken down into sections such as "Foundation," "Body," and "Finishing," amongst others.

**The Process of Understanding Instructions**

Putting a series of instructions inside of parentheses and brackets accomplishes the same purpose. For example, "(sc, 2dc) in next ch" means you will do all those stitches into one chain stitch.

These are the beginning and ending points of a sequence that will be repeated. They are denoted by an asterisk. If you see "*sc, hdc, dc*, repeat," you must repeat the sequence of sc, dc, and dc for the number of times indicated.

To "turn" something means to "flip" what you're working on and begin a new row.

Join is a term that is typically reserved for the conclusion of rounds and is used to connect the very last stitch to the very first.

**Work Even:** Proceed in the same manner as before, without altering the general pattern.

## Comparison of Charts and Written Patterns

There are patterns available that provide not only written instructions but also a chart. Charts are much easier to visualize than written instructions because they use symbols to represent the various types of stitches. On the other hand, written patterns can provide instructions with more nuances. If you want to have a complete understanding, using them together is a good rule of thumb.

## The Most Frequent Mistakes

**Skimming**: Before you get started on the project, make sure you take the time to read through the entire pattern. The most common cause for "frogging" (ripping out stitches, as in "rip it, rip it") is skipping lines while knitting or crocheting.

Not Keeping Track of Your Stitches It is important to keep track of your stitches, especially when beginning a row or round with a particular stitch count.

**Ignoring the Gauge:** We've already discussed this, but it's important enough to bring up again. Get your bearings under you!

Not Using a Safety Net When working on complicated patterns, it is recommended that you use a "lifeline," which is a piece of waste yarn that is threaded through your live stitches. If you make a mistake, it is simple to undo your work and return to the lifeline without sacrificing your progress.

**Advice for Achieving Victory**

Make Notes and Underline Important Steps Whether using a paper pattern or a digital copy, it's important to make notes and underline important steps.

You Should Consider YouTube a Companion: If you need help with a certain stitch or technique, there is probably a tutorial that can help you.

**Exercise:** If you need help with what to do, practice the difficult part on a test swatch first, then move on to the real thing.

**Participate in Online Forums:** If you need assistance or want to share your progress, joining an online community like Ravelry or a crochet-focused group on Facebook is a great option.

Sometimes, you will find a pattern you adore in large part, but there is one small detail you would like to alter. Once you have gained familiarity with reading patterns, it will be much simpler for you to make adjustments. Do you want a ruffle added? Don't be afraid to try. Would you rather have a different edging? Why shouldn't they? The pattern should be more of a principle than an absolute law. As soon as you fully grasp the fundamentals, you will be well on your way to personalizing projects so they are distinctively yours.

Reading crochet patterns can feel like learning a new language at first, but like any other language, it has its own set of benefits that come along with mastering it. Every new pattern that you master is comparable to a new conversation that you can have in a foreign language. It gives you more power, makes you feel fulfilled, and paves the way for infinite creative possibilities. Therefore, do not avoid the difficulty of the task. Rather than resisting it, give in to it and watch as your crocheting prowess skyrockets.

# Stitch Mastery

**Classic Crochet Stitches: Building Blocks of Design**

**Single, Half Double, Double, and Treble Crochet: Dive deep into these foundational stitches, covering variations and common uses.**

Cooking is similar to crocheting. You just need a few basic components; the dish's success depends on how you combine them. In the world of crocheting, the basic stitches such as single crochet (sc), half double crochet (dc), double crochet (dc), and treble crochet (tr) are crucial elements. In this article, we will closely examine these basic stitches and explore some intriguing variations. Additionally, we will explore how these stitches are commonly used by providing examples.

**Simple Chain (sc)**

**How to Do It:** Place hook into work, yarn over, pull up loop, yarn over again, and draw through both loops on the hook.

**Variations:** The extended single crochet (esc), which increases the stitch's height by adding an additional yarn over and pull-through step, is a relative of the single crochet.

**Common Applications:** Amigurumi (those adorable stuffed creatures), dishcloths, and other items requiring a dense fabric all benefit from single crochet. Due to its neatness and lack of fanout, it is often preferred for borders and edging.

**Crochet half double (hdc)**

**How to Do It:** Pull through all three loops on the hook by yarn over-ing, inserting, pulling up, and yarn over-ing the hook.

To add texture, the half-double crochet can also be worked in the front loop only (FLO) or the rear loop only (BLO). Additionally, there is "herringbone half double crochet," which uses a distinct pull-through technique and has a skewed appearance.

**Common Applications:** This stitch adds some drape and flexibility without producing an extremely holey cloth. It works well for clothes, blankets, and scarves.

**The dc (double crochet)**

The technique follows yarn over, insert hook, yarn over, pull up a loop, yarn over, and pull through two loops twice.

**Variations:** Because double crochet is tall, it is frequently used in V-stitch and shell patterns. The FPdc and BPdc create a raised texture but are more complex.

**Common Applications:** Double crochet is perfect for patterns that require a fluid drape since it offers faster height and a lighter texture, making it excellent for granny squares and shawls.

## Tr (treble crochet)

**How to Do It:** Insert hook, yarn over twice, pull up a loop, yarn over twice, pull through two loops, yarn over three times.

**Variations:** Extended treble crochet adds a second yarn-over and pull-through step to lengthen the stitch. You can also do front and back post-treble crochets like double crochet.

**Common Applications:** Treble crochet is frequently employed in lace patterns, openwork, and when dramatic draping is desired because of its height. Although it is less often than the other stitches, it is a jewel when you want to draw attention to yourself.

## The Foundations of Design

A staggering variety of textures and designs may be produced by combining these basic stitches in infinite ways. As an illustration, the "seed stitch" is a fundamental design that mixes single and double crochets. Looking to cause a stir? Mix shorter and taller stitches together in the same row.

Remember that once you're familiar with these fundamentals, you can experiment with variants to give your work more intricacy and flair. These stitches can create anything you can imagine in crochet, from straightforward dishcloths to elaborate lace shawls. Happy catching!

**Slip Stitch and Chain: Explore the versatility of these basic stitches in joining, edging, and creating texture.**

The slip stitch (sl st) and chain (ch) are like the unsung heroes or, you know, the drummers in a rock band when it comes to crochet. They frequently get overshadowed by fancier stitches, but they really are the Swiss Army knives of your crochet toolbox. Let's discuss why these fundamental stitches are the real MVPs in your crochet game because they are flexible, adaptive, and plain necessary.

**(Sl st) Slip Stitch**

Hook into stitch, yarn over, pull through stitch, and make a loop on hook to complete the stitch. You've slipped a stitch, bang!

**Versatility in Joining:** The slip stitch is your go-to partner for smoothly fusing rounds or stitches together. This stitch provides a neat and tight finish, whether you're finishing off a hat or making a loop handle for a bag.

Creating a clean edge or sewing two parts together without adding bulk is sometimes desired. For these activities, the slip stitch is a great option because it lies flat and doesn't add extra height.

Contrary to popular belief, textured fabric may be made using the simple slip stitch. Slip stitches are frequently used in techniques like Bosnian crochet to produce a dense and elastic fabric. Additionally, it is used in surface crochet to embellish finished pieces with patterns.

**(ch) chain**

Yarn over and pull through the loop on the hook are the steps to take. I'm done now! Those who are new to crocheting frequently start with this stitch.

Chain stitches are used as the foundation row in the majority of crochet creations. But that is not all that it does. Chains are frequently used in openwork and lace patterns to create space or act as "transitional" stitches by raising your yarn to the height of the following stitch (as in a turn).

When you encounter "ch-sp" (chain space) in a pattern, know that this tiny chain is doing important tasks like functioning as a stand-in for upcoming stitches or making a pretty hole in the cloth.

Have you heard about chain-loop mesh for making fabrics? The fabric is formed almost entirely of chains and slip stitches, making it lightweight and breathable. Ideal for producing sacks or summer clothing.

**They serve as both fundamentals and building blocks**

Beyond their 'basic' moniker, the slip stitch and chain are adaptable components that you can combine with other stitches to make a variety of textures, shapes, and motifs. Chain loops, for example, can make an edge frilly, while a slip stitch can sharply delineate a pattern.

Additionally, chains can be used to create jewelry, fringe, or drawstrings. Consider using slip stitches to make a tightly woven hot pad or chain arches to make a lacy shawl. There are absolutely countless options.

So, the next time you're hooking away, remember to acknowledge these sturdy stitches. Even though they might not always be the center of attention, stagehands are essential to any performance.

## Advanced Stitches: Elevating Your Craft

**Cluster, Bobble, and Puff Stitches: Techniques for creating texture and dimension in projects.**

You've learned the fundamentals and are now thinking, "Cool, but I need some pizzazz in my crochet life." The texture triumvirate has arrived: the Cluster, Bobble, and Puff stitches. These stitches are not your standard ones; they are the stitch equivalent of a flamboyant, complicated, and thoroughly enjoyable rock song guitar solo. Let's look at these complex stitches that make you look like a crochet whiz.

**Cluster Stitch**

**How it Works:** This is essentially a set of unfinished stitches that are worked into the same stitch or space and then finished together (possibly double crochet, treble crochet, etc.). In other words, you yarn over and pull through all the loops after leaving the last loop of each stitch on the hook.

**How to Use It:** Including texture without going overboard is a fantastic technique. Cluster stitches are frequently used to outline forms in more complicated patterns or to create floral designs. They are like the understated flair that ups your style game without shouting, "Look at me!"

**Bobble Stitch**

**How it Works:** Unlike clusters, a bobble is a collection of stitches (often double crochet) finished one at a time and linked at the top and bottom to form a, well, bobble. Each stitch is completed, but you link them together so that they stand out on the opposite side of your creation.

**How to Use It:** The life of the party is this stitch! Making a strong message is key. This stitch will entice people to reach out and touch your creation, making it ideal for adding 3D polka dots to cushions or introducing tactile interest to baby blankets. It's like embellishing your crochet with exclamation points!

**Puff Stitch**

The procedure follows Yarn over, insert hook into stitch, Yarn over again, and draw loop up. Repeat this procedure a few times before yarning over and drawing through all the loops on the hook.

**How to Use It:** Unlike bobbles and clusters, puff stitches give a softer, airier feel. They are ideal for lightweight, breathable, yet textural items because they add volume without weight. Think of the froth on your cappuccino or a puffy cloud draped across a shawl.

Each stitch is a high note in your project's symphony.

**Front and Back Post Stitches: Methods to achieve raised patterns and ribbing effects.**

Front and Back Post Stitches are your go-to techniques to make your crochet work stand out—literally. These stitches give your creations depth, texture, and visual fascination, just like the special effects team in a big-budget film. So, let's examine how to perform these two stitches and their intended applications.

**(FPS) Front Post Stitch**

**Instructions:**

1. To begin a double crochet, yarn over once (unless another foundation stitch is used).
2. As if hugging it from the front, wrap your hook around the stitch's 'post' from the row below.
3. Make a loop with yarn and draw it up. On the hook, there will be three loops.
4. Pull through the first two loops after reversing the yarn.
5. Reverse the yarn and pull it through the final two loops. Voila! You've finished stitching a Front Post.

**Uses and Results:** The side of the fabric facing you develops a ridge or bump due to FPS. This works wonders for highlighting cable patterns, providing sweaters ribbed edges, and adding tactile appeal to blankets. The raised stitches can create intriguing geometrical designs when used in conjunction with ordinary stitches.

**(BPS) Back Post Stitch**

**Instructions:**

1. To get ready for a double crochet (or equivalent basic stitch), yarn over.
2. This time, insert the hook from the back of the work and move it to the front before wrapping it around the stitch post and returning it to the back.
3. Now that you have three loops on the hook, yarn over and draw up a loop.
4. Pull the yarn through two loops and re-yarn.
5. Reverse the yarn and pass it through the final two loops. Just now, you completed a Back Post Stitch.

Uses and Results BPS complements the elevated portions made by FPS by making an indentation or depression on the side of the fabric facing you. Suppose you want to make textured, three-dimensional fabric. In that case, this stitch is ideal for a complex afghan or an article of distinctive clothing.

These stitches can be combined to create a world of textured wonders. Consider FPS and BPS the peanut butter and jelly of crochet: each is great on its own, but when combined, they produce something truly exceptional.

**Shell and Fan Stitches: Delicate designs often used for intricate patterns and lacy effects.**

When you enter the realm of crochet lace, Shell and Fan Stitches are bound to come your way. These are the crochet world's prima donnas, renowned for their delicate designs and light textures. These stitches, which are frequently seen showing off on shawls, wraps, and sentimental afghans, lend either a vintage charm or a modern refinement, depending on how you employ them. Here is an explanation:

**Shutter Stitch**

**Instructions:**

1. To place the hook in the appropriate stitch, yarn over.
2. Make a loop with yarn and draw it up.
3. Two loops are left on your hook after yarning over and drawing through two loops. This double crochet is unfinished.
4. Four more times in the same stitch, repeat steps 1-3.
5. The hook will have six loops. Pull the yarn through each of the six loops.
6. Use a chain stitch to affix the Shell.

**Uses and Results:** Although shell stitches are frequently employed in borders, they can produce stunning all-over fabrics. They are excellent for giving normally straight, linear crochet curves and waves. The feminine touch added by this pattern makes it a great choice for baby blankets, shawls, and summer shirts.

**A fan stitch**

**Instructions:**

1. Using the designated stitch, double crochet.
2. One chain.
3. Into the same stitch, double crochet.
4. To achieve the required fan width, repeat steps 2 and 3. Form fans by spacing 5 double crochets apart with chains.
5. Chain or create a close stitch, such as a single crochet, in the following stitch to finish the fan.

**Uses and Results:** Fan stitches offer your fabric a light, airy feel and semicircular appearance. These fabrics are preferred for shawls, lacy tops, and delicate house accents like table runners or drapes. The fan stitch's openwork enables for a softer, more fluid drape.

The Shell and Fan Stitches both extend an invitation to explore the realm of more complex crochet patterns. Your crafts might become poetic by successfully utilizing them; they're like crochet's ritzy vocabulary. So, whether you're trying to make a garment that screams "sophistication" or a home piece that whispers "elegance," these stitches are your reliable partners.

## Techniques for Shaping and Joining

**Increasing and Decreasing: Techniques to shape projects, essential for garments and three-dimensional items.**

Let's face it: not everything in crochet is a square or rectangle. Shape-changing strategies like rising and decreasing are essential to boost your game. Knowing how to increase and decrease is essential whether you're making a 3D amigurumi, a snug cap, or a fitting sweater. Let's begin, then.

**Increasing**

Adding more stitches to a row or circle to make it wider is the definition of increasing. It's the fashion designer of the crochet world, constantly giving things style and shape. The following describes how to increase simple stitches like single crochet (sc):

**Single crochet increases (sc inc) instructions:**

1. A hook should be inserted into the stitch that has to be increased.
2. Make a loop with yarn and draw it up.
3. Pull the yarn through the two loops on the hook and re-yarn.

4.  In the exact same stitch, repeat steps 1-3.

## Uses and Results

Increases are frequently employed to add room or enlarge the rounds of hats or the bust regions of clothing. Additionally, while creating granny squares or hexagons, they are useful in the corners to prevent the design from curling up.

## Decreasing

Decreasing requires joining two or more stitches together to make your creation smaller. It is essentially the inverse of increasing. Consider it as your project's personal trainer, constantly working to get tighter and leaner.

## Single crochet decrease (sc dec) instructions:

1.  Hook up by inserting it into the first stitch.
2.  Make a loop with yarn and draw it up.
3.  Hook up to the subsequent stitch.
4.  Pull up another loop by yarning once more.
5.  On the hook, there will be three loops. Pull through all three by using yarn.

## Uses and Results

The top of a cap or the waist of a sweater are both shaped by decreasing. Making the shapes that result in miniature animals, dolls, and other amusing creatures is also crucial for amigurumi.

The ability to increase and decrease is a true skill that improves the functionality and appearance of your work. Once you've mastered them, you can influence your crochet universe little by little.

**Seaming Methods: Different ways to join crocheted pieces, including slip stitch join, single crochet join, and the mattress stitch.**

Now that you have all these exquisitely crocheted pieces, it's time to perform a Frankenstein and sew them together to create a work of art. Seaming is used in this situation. Seaming can make or break the appearance and durability of your finished item; it's not just about slamming things together. Let's explore popular techniques, including the mattress stitch, single crochet connect and slip stitch join.

## Slip-stitch joining

Slip stitches are similar to the sneaky ninjas of crochet. They are understated but effective at keeping things together.

## Instructions:

1. Hold your two pieces in a side-by-side or stacked position.
2. Where you want to begin, pierce both layers of stitches with the hook.
3. Re-yarn and pass the yarn through each loop.
4. Along the length of your pieces, repeat steps 2 and 3.

**Uses and effects:** The slip stitch connect adds only a small amount of bulk to your product, making it perfect for projects where you desire a clean aesthetic, such as combining granny squares.

## Single Crochet Join

The single crochet joint is your go-to when you want a robust seam that adds some design.

## Instructions:

1. Your components can be arranged vertically or horizontally.

2. Wherever you want to begin, insert your hook between the stitches.

3. Pull through both loops on the hook after yarning over, pulling up a loop, and then yarning over again.

4. Continue for the duration of the pieces.

**Uses and Results:** This technique creates a ridge that can be buried on your work's "wrong" side or used as a decorative element on the "right" side.

**Mattress Stapling**

Ah, the mattress stitch offers a practically imperceptible join and is the seamstress of the crochet world.

**Instructions:**

1. With some yarn, thread a knitting needle.

2. Hold the pieces so that the right sides are up.

3. Along the seam, weave the yarn in and out of the edge stitches on each piece.

4. To bring the edges together, lightly tighten.

**Uses and Results:** The mattress stitch is perfect for clothing or any item where a discrete seam is important. You now have three tried-and-true seaming techniques to add to your crochet toolbox. They focus on improving your full component rather than just joining.

**Working in the Round: Methods and best practices for crocheting in circular patterns, essential for hats, amigurumi, and certain blanket designs.**

Working in the round is the way to boost your crochet game. It's essential to creating hats, amigurumi, and several stylish blanket patterns. Circular motion, however, requires some delicacy to maintain everything looking and feeling appropriate; it's more complex than it would seem.

## Chain Method vs. Magic Circle

A must-know for amigurumi and challenging tasks is the Magic Circle.

**Instructions:**

1. Make a loop with your yarn as directed.
2. Hook up to the loop with your hook.
3. Chain one (or more, depending on your stitch) by pulling up a loop.
4. Stitch into the loop from the first round of stitches.
5. Tighten the loop.

**Chain Method:** Effective when a loose center is acceptable.

**Instructions:**

1. Chain three to four stitches, as directed.
2. A slip stitch is used to connect the last and initial chains.
3. Work the initial round into the chain loop's middle.
4. Getting bigger each round

When working in the round, you must either reduce to make things easier or raise to maintain things flat. Typically, increases are made by combining two stitches from the preceding round.

**Slip Stitch vs. Continuous Rounds for Joins**

**Sliding Stitch Join:**

Slip stitch into the first stitch of each round to finish it, then chain one to begin the next.

**Rounds That Continue:**

Put a stitch marker in the first stitch of the previous round and work the first stitch of the subsequent round right into it.}

**Advice and Ideal Methods**

**Keep Count:** Mark the beginning of each round with a stitch marker.

Concerning tension, Maintain constant tension, especially when performing complex patterns.

**Trial and error:** Perfecting a skill takes practice. Test out various approaches to find which one suits your project the best.

Working in the round is crucial for shaping and linking your creations, whether making a warm beanie, an amigurumi animal, or a circular blanket. Prepare your hooks, grab some yarn, and start a circle!

## Colorwork and Patterns in Crochet

**Tapestry Crochet: Techniques for carrying multiple yarns to create intricate color patterns.**

Intricate color patterns perfect for Instagram may be made with tapestry crochet, like the cool cousin of normal crochet. With this method, you work while carrying around many yarns, creating a dense, textured fabric with astounding patterns. If you have yet to try your hand at tapestry crochet, you're really losing out.

**Basics: Carrying Yarn**

**Start with a Base:** Work a few stitches in a base color to provide the groundwork for your project.

**Adding a Second Color:** To add a new color, simply put the new yarn over the stitches and continue crocheting over it. This will effectively conceal the new color in your work.

**Color Change:** Work till the last yarn-over of the previous stitch before finishing the stitch with the new color to switch colors.

**Techniques to Master**

The preferred stitch for crocheting tapestries is single crochet. It maintains the integrity of your work and offers more control over color changes.

Let the secondary color "float" along the back or inside the stitches with floating yarn when not in use. You will pick it up when it's time to switch colors.

**Texture and tension**

To best disguise the yarn you're carrying, keep your stitches tight. The negative? Your writing can start to curl. To avoid this, experiment with a larger hook for the carrying yarn or slightly looser tension.

**Starting Simple**

If you've never crocheted a tapestry, start with straightforward geometric patterns. If you're feeling ambitious, try more challenging designs like florals, waves, or characters once you've gotten the hang!

**Quick Instructions**

**Choosing Colors:** For optimum impact, choose two or more contrasting colors.

**Get Your Pattern Ready:** Use a pre-made graph or make one of your own.

**Beginning crocheting:** Make the foundation chain using your base color.

**Bring in a new color:** Be careful to bring the unused color with you as you bring the second color in.

**Maintain Your Graph:** Use the pattern or graph to choose when to change colors.

Tapestry crochet is a thrilling way to up your crafting game because it offers countless customization and creative possibilities. So go ahead and start crocheting with those numerous yarn balls!

**Jacquard Crochet: Methods for two-color designs that create stunning visuals.**

Jacquard crochet is where you enhance your colorwork skills. This approach is your jam if you're all about intricate, two-color patterns that make folks go, "Whoa, how'd you do that?" Made from conventional weaving techniques, Jacquard crochet enables you to produce stunning images that give even simple designs a high-end feel.

**Jacquard 101**

Choose two contrasting colors for your two yarns; you'll work with both simultaneously.

**Only the right side:** With Jacquard, you mostly work on the fabric's right side, which prevents you from turning your work.

**Color Changes:** When you switch between your two yarns in the middle of a stitch, magic happens.

**Key Methods:**

It's essential to maintain tension. Your pattern will appear wavy or deformed if the tension is uneven.

**Invisible Joins:** Start the stitch with the working color and end it with the new color to make color changes appear seamless.

The yarn that isn't being used will "float" down the back. Keep these floats loose; otherwise, the drape of your product will suffer.

**Detailed Guidelines:**

The foundation row is as easy as making a chain stitch with your primary color (Color A).

**Introduce Secondary Color:** Do not chop off Color A; you will deal with both colors. Instead, introduce your secondary color (Color B).

**Initial Stitch:** Use Color A to begin your first stitch. Pull up a loop after inserting your hook into the stitch and yarning over.

Change colors before finishing the stitch by dropping Color A and picking up Color B.

**Repeat the pattern:** Follow the pattern you've chosen, being careful to change colors as directed. Maintain the two yarns in the back of your project.

Before continuing to the next row or finishing off, ensure all your floats are uniform and your stitches are nice.

Although jacquard crochet requires care and concentration, the outcome is well worth it. The options are boundless, ranging from intricate themes to breathtaking visual tapestries. With this technique, you can truly showcase your craftsmanship by transforming commonplace undertakings into remarkable works of art. Pick your colors now, and let the hook speak for itself!

**Intarsia Crochet: Working with patches of color, especially useful for graphghan blankets.**

With intarsia crochet, each color combines a distinct brushstroke to form a picture or design. This method is a winner if you enjoy creating graphghan blankets, wall hangings, or other items that call for exact color arrangement.

**What's Basic:**

**Color Blocks:** Using several color blocks is the foundation of intarsia. A bobbin or miniature ball of yarn is provided for each color segment.

**One Side at a Time:** You typically only work on the right side to keep your color blocks organized and distinct.

**No Carrying:** Yarn is not carried behind the work, unlike crocheting for tapestries or jacquards. Every color block stands alone.

**Key Methods:**

Tension is Your Friend: To prevent distorting your pattern, make sure your stitches are uniform.

Manage your bobbins by keeping them all free of tangles. You want to avoid a tricky issue in the middle!

**Color Change:** Pick up the new color and complete the stitch with it when you are ready to switch colors and are at the last yarn-over of a stitch.

**Detailed Guidelines:**

**Lay the Groundwork:** Chain the necessary number of stitches for your row using your primary color (in this case, let's say Color A).

**Get Your Bobbins Ready:** Your other colors can be divided into little balls or wind tiny amounts onto bobbins.

**Change Colors:** Finish the last yarn-over of the current stitch with the new color as you reach a color change in your pattern.

**Drop-Off and Pick-Up:** As you take up the new color, put down the one you just used, keeping your tension constant.

**Continue Crocheting:** As you continue, change colors as necessary. Keep in mind that each color should come from a separate bobbin.

**Finish:** After finishing each row or round, cut the yarn, leaving a long tail for subsequent weaving.

Once you get the hang of it, intarsia crochet can be immensely satisfying, even though it initially seems intimidating. Preparation and mindfulness are essential. You'll quickly become an expert at creating vibrant crochet mosaics if you keep your bobbins arranged and keep the tension constant. So, let's make some art and snag that hook!

## Special Techniques: Beyond the Basics

**Tunisian Crochet: A unique method that combines elements of knitting and crochet.**

The greatest aspects of knitting and conventional crochet are combined in a beautiful Tunisian crochet. The outcome? Beautifully textured, wonderfully flexible fabric that begs for your imagination. This method uses a unique hook called the Tunisian Crochet Hook, which is longer than a standard crochet hook and can handle numerous loops simultaneously. It has countless uses, but producing thick, cuddly blankets is one of its best uses.

**What's Basic:**

The fundamental stitch in Tunisian crochet is known as the Tunisian Simple Stitch (TSS).

**Forward and Return Pass:** In contrast to traditional crochet, each row comprises a "forward pass," where loops are gathered on the hook, and a "return pass," where the loops are worked off.

**Never Turn:** Yes, you never turn your Tunisian crochet work!

**Key Methods:**

Maintaining consistent tension is more essential in crochet than in other styles.

Keep your stitches loose unless the pattern specifies otherwise because the fabric can become constrictive.

Tunisian crochet is a great technique for colorwork. Feel free to mix and match!

**Detailed Guidelines:**

1.  Chain the necessary amount of stitches according to your pattern to start.
2.  **Forward Pass:** Yarn over and pull up a loop while hooking onto the second chain from the hook. Holding the loops on the hook, keep pulling up loops from each chain.
3.  **Return Pass:** Yarn over and pull through two loops, then yarn over and pull through the first loop to form a chain. Once you have one loop on your hook, keep drawing through the two loops.

4. **Tunisian Simple Stitch (Tss):** Insert your hook beneath the vertical bar of the subsequent stitch in the subsequent row, yarn over it, and pull up a loop. Continue across.

5. **Proceed with the process:** Follow your pattern and stitch type as you continue to do the forward and backward passes until your product is finished.

6. **Bind Off:** To complete, place your hook in the same location as you would for a Tss, but instead of leaving the loop on the hook, draw it through the loop that is already there, basically making a slip stitch.

**Broomstick Lace: Using a large knitting needle or dowel to create beautiful lacy designs.**

A crochet technique known as "broomstick lace" takes your cloth to a nearly mystical level. Surprisingly, a large knitting needle or dowel can also create this elaborate pattern in addition to a crochet hook.

**You'll require:**

- Hook for crocheting, sized for the pattern
- Dowels or large knitting needles (20–25 mm in diameter)

**How to Execute:**

1. **Basic Loop:** To begin, draw up a sizable loop from the crocheted fabric and set it on the dowel. This is the loop on your broomstick.

2. Continuing the process of gathering loops, place them on the dowel from each stitch in your row. There should be several loops.

3. **Loop Transfer:** Carefully remove the loops from the dowel, then thread your crochet hook through the first set of loops (often 4-5 loops, depending on the pattern).

4. **Safe and Sound:** Pull the yarn through the loops and re-knit. With one crochet, they are held together. You can add more stitches, like double crochet, depending on your pattern.
5. **Repeat:** For each group of loops across the row, repeat this procedure.
6. **The last touch:** Under the instructions, finish your row by securing the final set of loops with a regular crochet stitch.
7. **Next Row:** For a more diverse texture, continue with more Broomstick Lace rows or change to a different stitch.

Broomstick Lace is flexible because of the contrasting textures of solid crochet and open lacy loops. It works well for creating shawls, afghans, and scarves. Once you try it, the ethereal designs you can make will astound you.

**Hairpin Lace: Working with a hairpin lace loom to produce delicate, looped patterns.**

Crocheting with hairpin lace gives your projects a distinctive flair and allows for light, delicate motifs. It uses a unique hairpin lace loom apparatus to make looped cloth strips. These strips may be combined to create intricate, web-like designs ideal for shawls, scarves, and chic clothing accents.

**You'll require:**

- The hairpin lace loom
- Hook for crocheting (size depends on project)
- Yarn (of your choosing; lighter yarns frequently produce the best results)

**How to Execute:**

**Setting up the Loom:** Change the width of your loops on your hairpin lace loom. The loops get bigger as the setting gets broader.

**Initial Loop:** To create the first loop, tie a slip knot, then insert your crochet hook through the loop on one side of the loom prong.

**Making the Initial Loop:** Take the yarn from behind the loom's second prong, bring it to the front, and loop it around the crochet hook.

**Establishing the Loop:** Pull through the loop on the hook by yarn-over-ing. You've just completed your first loop of hairpin lace.

**Rotation:** To reset your position and start the loop-making process, turn the loom 180 degrees.

**Repeat:** Continue looping and spinning the loom while ensuring that there are equal loops on each side.

**Removal from Loom:** Carefully slide the loops of the loom's prongs once you've finished the strip or the desired amount of loops.

**Connecting Strips:** To combine several strips to create a fabric, you can use a variety of crochet stitches, including single crochet, slip stitch, and even more intricate ones.

**Finish:** Add a row of single crochet to the top and bottom of your work to create a neat edge.

Hairpin lace can appear intimidating at first, but after you master balancing the loom and crochet hook, you'll discover it's a method that's incredibly satisfying. It enables you to explore a completely new level of texture and design, giving your work a dash of elegant sophistication.

# Blueprints in Yarn

## Granny Square Blanket

The Granny Square Blanket is a timeless classic in the crochet community, comparable to the ultimate comfort meal. Let's get started by learning how to make one.

**You'll require:**

- Multiple-color yarn (weakest weight suggested)
- Crochet hook size 5 mm (or the hook size necessary for your yarn)
- Scissors, yarn needles

**Step-by-Step Guidelines**

**Decide on Your Colors:** There are no boundaries. Choose between bold colors, a monochromatic palette, or everything in between.

**Individual Squares: Making:**

1. Chaining 6 and connecting a ring with a slip stitch to make a ring. Next, chain 3 (this will serve as the first double crochet), then work 2 double crochets into the ring and chain 2. This will result in 2 chains and 3 double crochets inside the ring. Repeat this process until you reach the top of the first chain 3, then join it with a slip stitch.
2. Round 2: Slip stitch to the first corner gap of the chain-2 chain. In the same spot, chain 3, 2 double crochets, and chain 2, 3 double crochets. In the following chain-2 space, chain 1 is followed by three double crochets. Repetition is encouraged.
3. Size Does Matter: Set the size of each square; you may either stop after two rounds or continue until the size you want is achieved.

**Squares to be counted:** Determine the layout, whether 10x10 or 20x20 squares, based on the size of the blanket you wish to make.

**Become a Square:**

Place the squares face down on a flat surface to organize your arrangement.

1. Row by row, link them with a single crochet or a slip stitch.
2. Join yarn at any corner to create an edge.
3. Around the blanket, single crochet each stitch.
4. Try a picot or scalloped edge for a nicer edge.

**Decorative touches:** With your yarn needle, cut the yarn, fasten it, and weave in all the annoying ends.

Voilà! You now possess a special, colorful Granny Square blanket that fits you well. Feel free to add stitches or embellishments to liven up the garments; these instructions are only suggestions.

## Amigurumi Toys

The Japanese specialty of making tiny, stuffed yarn animals and things is amigurumi. Amigurumi transforms yarn into tiny marvels, from adorable animals to imaginative food items and personalities. What could be better than homemade, fuzzy crochet toys?

**You'll require:**

- Worsted weight yarn in your choice of colors
- crochet hook, size 3.5
- Filler made of fibers
- Sticky notes
- Knit needle
- Safety eyes may be used.

**Basic Procedures for Making Amigurumi Toys:**

**Plan and Design:** Choose the creation you wish to make. If you're feeling creative, draw up a straightforward design.

**Beginning of the project**

The majority of amigurumi begin with a magic ring.

1. Create a loop and leave a lengthy tail for working with. Hook into the loop in the middle, yarn over, and pull through. Round 1 stitches should be worked into the ring.
2. 6 single crochet (SC) stitches are placed into the magic ring in round 1.

## Building Form

1. Round 2: Increase (12 stitches) by making two SCs in each stitch.
2. Round 3: One SC, increase, and repeat (18 stitches).
3. To widen the form, keep adding stitches every round. To build length, single crochet without adding stitches.
4. When building an animal, you would add safety eyes or sew on a face at this point.
5. Fill the form with fiberfill stuffing before sealing it up. Use a stick or the pencil's back to squeeze through narrow spaces.

**Closing Up:** Start decreasing (SC 2 stitches together) and continue until the shape can be closed.

**Adding the finishing touches:** If your amigurumi has limbs, ears, or other features, make them separately and sew them with a yarn needle. Leave a long tail after cutting the yarn to complete. Pull firmly after threading this through the remaining stitches. Gather all loose ends and secure them.

You've just created your very own amigurumi toy—congrats! The specifics will vary depending on what you're making, but these are the fundamentals that all amigurumi have. Be inventive, and most importantly, enjoy yourself!

# Market Tote Bag

Do disposable plastic bags make your life a mess? How about using strong cotton yarn to make a long-lasting, green-market tote bag? You're not just minimizing waste but also making something wholly original. Crochet totes are fashionable now, so you can kill two birds with one stone!

**You'll require:**

- Worsted-weight cotton yarn is a good option.

- 5-millimeter crochet hook
- knit needle
- Sticky notes

## How to Make a Market Tote Bag in Crochet:

30 stitches should be chained to form the foundation chain. This will determine the width of your bag, so make the necessary adjustments if you want a larger or smaller tote.

## Beginning of the Bag:

1. Row 1: SC in the second chain from the hook and across each chain, turning after each SC.
2. Chain 1, work an SC in each stitch across, then turn.
3. For about 15 rows, repeat Row 2 to build a solid foundation.

## Bag's Main Body:

4. Chain 3 (this counts as the first double crochet, or DC), then DC in each stitch across, turning after each DC.
5. Row 2: Chain 4 (counts as first DC and chain 1), skip the next stitch, DC in the next, chain 1; repeat throughout, ending with a DC in the last stitch, turn.
6. Chain 3, DC across each DC, chain gap, then turn.
7. Rows 2 and 3 should be alternated until the bag is the appropriate height.
8. Handle Row 1: Chain 1, SC in first five stitches, chain 20 (or more for a longer handle), skip 20 stitches, SC in next ten stitches, chain 20, skip 20 stitches, SC in last five threads, turn.
9. Chain 1, SC in each stitch, and chain across for row two.
10. For a strong handle, repeat Row 2 for an additional 3–5 times.

**Finishing:** Cut the yarn and weave in all loose ends with a needle.

# Infinity Scarf

Nothing is as cozy or fashionable as an infinity scarf when the chill creeps in. One or two loops around your neck will give you instant warmth and style points. Crocheting an infinity scarf is a simple craft that even novices can do. You may use thicker yarn for a more delicate touch or chunkier yarn for a cozier feel.

**You'll require:**

- Choose your preferred yarn (thick for a warm scarf, thin for a delicate one).
- Use a crochet hook appropriate for your yarn (check the label).
- knit needle
- Stitch markers if they are available.

**How to Make an Infinity Scarf with Crochet:**

1. Starting Chain: Depending on the yarn you've chosen, chain enough stitches for the chain to comfortably circle around your neck after it's attached. You might begin with 80 chains for chunky yarn and approximately 150 for thinner yarn.
2. Break the Chain: Slip stitch the initial chain together to form a circle. If you'd like, mark the beginning of your rounds with a stitch marker at this point.
3. Chain 2 in the first round (this qualifies as your first HDC). HDC all the way around in each chain. To join, slip the stitch into the top of the second chain.
4. Chain 3 in the second round for your first double crochet (DC). DC around the entire stitch. To join, slip the stitch into the third chain from the top.
5. Continue: You have the option of continuing to alternate between rounds of HDC and rounds of DC, or you may decide to use just one stitch throughout the entire scarf. It's up to you! Just keep in mind to use slip stitches to join each round.

**Finishing:** Cut your yarn, leaving a long tail, once you've reached the appropriate width. Use your yarn needle to weave in all exposed ends to give it a tidy finish.

There you have it, then! A stylish, cozy, and personalized infinity scarf. This is a great item to add to your winter wardrobe or give as a beautiful present.

## Barefoot Sandals

For yoga classes, beach outings, and garden relaxation, barefoot sandals are your feet's best friends. These toe and ankle loops for feet offer a chic alternative to be 'barefoot' while also accessorizing your feet. They are fashionable and can easily be individualized in color, design, and bead accents.

**You'll require:**

- Cotton Yarn (Cotton is breathable and machine washable.)
- Hook for crochet (size will depend on the gauge of the yarn; often, a 4mm or 5mm hook would do)
- Decoration beads or charms (optional)
- Knit needle

**How to Make Your Own Barefoot Sandals with Crochet:**

1. Toe Loop: Begin by chaining 20 stitches (modify this to your toe size; 20 stitches should easily fit around a big toe). To create a loop, slip stitch to the first chain.
2. Foot ornamentation: To begin your first double crochet (DC), chain 3. Slip stitch to the third chain of the beginning chain 3 after adding 19 additional DCs into the loop. This results in a tiny circle.
3. Construct the Design: Here, you can be imaginative! A typical following round involves chaining three (as the first DC), placing one DC in each stitch surrounding it, and then attaching a chain of three to five stitches that loops back into the original thread to form a little picot. Completely complete the circle, then attach it with a slip stitch.

4. Chain enough stitches to comfortably encircle your ankle with an ankle strap. Depending on the size of your ankle and the yarn's elasticity, this might be anywhere from 60 to 100 stitches. Once finished, fasten this chain to the side of the foot circle that faces the opposite direction.

5. Decorate: If you want to add beads, you can either weave them in along the ankle strap or the foot circle or sew them on with a yarn needle later.

6. Finish: Cut the yarn and weave the ends using your yarn needle as soon as you are satisfied with the size and decorating.

You are now prepared to leave in style! Whether heading to the beach or just lounging on your lawn, your feet will look amazing.

## Baby Booties

The prettiest little crochet items you can work on are baby booties. They are easy to make and a thoughtful and useful gift for new or soon-to-be parents. These little treasures will make people smile, whether you choose soft or vivid hues, straightforward patterns, or complex ones.

**You'll require:**

- Soft baby yarn is recommended; mixtures of acrylic and cotton work well.
- Crochet hook (4mm is a common size; the size will depend on your yarn)
- Sticky notes
- knit needle
- Decoration buttons or ribbon (optional)

**Detailed crochet patterns for baby booties**

1. To begin, chain 20 stitches to create the first row. This will serve as the booty's foundation. Make sure the chain is flexible and tight enough.

2. The toe's shape: Beginning with the second chain from the hook, single crochet (SC) in each chain stitch for Row 1. Turn.

3. Chain 1, then SC across every stitch in row two. Turn.

4. Row 2 should be repeated four more times or until the desired toe height is achieved.

5. Establishing the Sides: SC in the following 10 stitches after the first chain. Turn.

6. Continue until the sides are tall enough to enclose the infant's foot snugly. Usually, 8–10 rows are required.

7. Fold your piece in half, aligning the side rows to form the heel. The heel can be closed by slipping stitching or SC-ing through both layers.

8. Pick up the area around the ankle opening and SC. For a decorative edge, add one or two picot stitches.

9. Straps: Construct a short chain that crosses the opening from one side to the other. Make a chain loop or leave a space between SCs to add a buttonhole. On the opposing side, fasten a button.

10. Finishing touches: If you decorate with ribbons or buttons, it is time to sew them on. When finished, use a yarn needle to weave in any remaining ends.

## Potholders and Dishcloths

The realm of crochet is a fantastic place to start with projects like potholders and dishcloths. They are very useful in the kitchen and provide a canvas on which to practice various stitches and techniques. Additionally, they make wonderful presents or even goods for a craft market.

**You'll require:**

- Cotton yarn (which is heat-resistant and absorbent)
- Crochet hook (5mm is a good starting point)
- Scissors
- Knit needle

**Simple Dishcloth Instructions:**

1. Start Simple: To make the foundation row, chain 30 stitches.
2. Single crochet (SC) across the first row after turning, starting at the second chain from the hook.
3. Make a texture: Chain 1, then pivot. Half double crochet (HDC) should be used for the entire row. Turn.
4. Repeat: The SC and HDC rows should be alternated until your piece is square.
5. Finish: Chain 1 and work SC evenly around the edges for a neater appearance after the last row. Trim the yarn, then weave the ends in.
6. Instructions for using a potholder:
7. Chain 25 stitches to lay the foundations.
8. Initial Row: Double crochet (DC) around and into the third chain from the hook.
9. Add Complications: Turn and chain three. To produce a textured design, combine SC and DC. An example would be SC, DC, SC in the same stitch, skip two stitches, and repeat.
10. Bulk Up: Work similarly until the piece is almost square, then work in SC for the final two rows.
11. Make a Loop Chain 10 when you get to the final stitch, then slip the stitch back into it to create a loop for hanging.
12. Finish by cutting the yarn, pulling it through, and weaving in any remaining ends.

Both tasks may be completed quickly and have lots of customization options. Do you want to add a border or try a more elaborate stitch? Try it out!

## Beanie or Slouchy Hat

Few crocheted items can match a beanie or slouchy hat in terms of combining fashion and usefulness. These hats are a wonderful way to demonstrate crocheting prowess, experiment with various stitches, and use different color combinations. They are suitable for all ages and are easily customizable. You'd like to inject some humor. Attach a pom-pom to the top!

**What You Will Need Is:**

- Worsted weight yarn (between 200 and 250 yards)
- A 5mm (H-8) crochet hook
- Scissors
- A yarn needle
- Optional: A basic beanie with poms.

**Instructions:**

1. Making a magic ring is the first step; the second is the first double crochet or DC.
2. To the magic ring, first round, add an additional 11 DC. The round is finished by adding a slip stitch to the top of the second chain.
3. Increase: Chain two for the second round, then insert two DCs into each stitch all the way around. Be sure to slip stitch at the conclusion.
4. For the third round of texturing, chain 2, then DC once in the first stitch, 2 DC in the next stitch, and so on. Rounding off using a slip stitch.
5. Build the Hat: When the diameter snugly fits around the head, continue with the design, adding more single DCs (2 DCs in one stitch) between the increases with each round.
6. Straight Rounds: Chain 2 and DC in each stitch all the way around, without increasing, until the hat is the desired length.
7. To complete, trim the yarn and weave in all the ends. If you want, add a pom-pom.

Potential Changes:

8. Texture: To create texture, you can change your stitch after your rounds of increasing by using the half-double crochet or front-post double crochet, for example.
9. For a striped look, switch up the yarn color every few rows.
10. Slouchy Hat: To give a hat a slouchy appearance, add straight rounds to make it longer.

Making your own crocheted hat allows you to customize its appearance and fit, which is one of its many benefits. The styling options are unlimited, whether you want a traditional beanie or a current slouchy hat!

## Lacy Shawl or Wrap

A beautiful finishing touch to any outfit is a lacy shawl or wrap that gives warmth without adding bulk and elegance with finesse. With this project, you may exercise your crochet skills with intricate stitch patterns and delicate decorations. With the ideal combination of yarn and stitch, lace crochet is lovely and transforms your creation into wearable art.

**You'll require:**

- Yarn that is fingering weight or lace weight (between 400 and 600 yards)
- Use an E-4 to a 4.5mm crochet hook, depending on the pattern and yarn.
- Sticky notes
- Scissors
- Knit needle

**Instructions for a Simple Lacy Shawl:**

1. Making a slip knot, chain 60 (or any other multiple of the pattern repeat) chains.
2. Turn and double crochet (DC) across, beginning with the third chain from the hook.

3. Pattern Rows: From now on, stick with your chosen lace stitch pattern. The fan stitch, pineapple stitch, and shell pattern are popular choices.

4. Turning and Increasing: In chain 3 (the first DC of the following row), turn your work at the end of each row and repeat the pattern. Increase stitches at the beginning and end of rows to make the shawl wider.

5. Repeat: Keep repeating the pattern rows until the desired length is reached.

6. Finishing touches: When satisfied with the size, add a delicate scalloped or pivoted border. Cut the yarn, secure it, and weave the ends together.

7. Optional Changes:

8. Using gradient yarn or switching colors every few rows will provide a refined touch.

9. Beadwork: Add beads for a touch of added flair. Before you begin, thread beads onto your yarn; then, as you work, include them.

10. Fringe: Add a fringe to the ends to give your shawl a boho-chic appearance.

A lacy shawl, whether one you make for yourself or as a gift, is an heirloom-caliber item that will dazzle. Each shawl you make is a one-of-a-kind manifestation of your talent and creativity because there are countless stitch combinations and design options.

## Home Decor

Crochet may revitalize your home decor in addition to being used for wearables. Crocheted objects add a warm, inviting atmosphere to any living space, whether a soft pillow cover, a detailed table runner, or a straightforward pair of coasters. Additionally, it's a wonderful chance to display your creativity and sense of style in a stunning and useful method.

**You'll require:**

- Your preferred yarn, cotton, is quite durable.
- suitable crochet hook size for your yarn
- Scissors

- Knit needle
- Tape measure

**Simple Pillow Cover Directions:**

1. Measure Your Pillow: To create a pillow cover, determine the pillow's dimensions first.
2. Construct two rectangular panels the same size as your pillow should be crocheted. For a dense texture, use a single crochet; for a softer feel, use double crochet.
3. Become a Panelist: Invert the two panels so their incorrect sides face one another. Single crochet across three of the edges to join them.
4. Place the pillow here: Insert your pillow before stapling the fourth side.
5. Finish: Around the final edge, continue to single crochet; when finished, fasten off and weave in ends.

**Ideas for Table Runners**

1. Select a Pattern: Pick a stitch pattern that you like. Attractive table runners can be made using the granny square or chevron patterns.
2. Determine the Width and Length: Choose the dimensions, then adjust the chain.
3. Craft: Continue stitching to your pattern until your table runner is the right length.

**Coaster guidelines:**

1. Create a magic ring to begin.
2. Chain three (counts as a double crochet) in the first round, then work 11 double crochets into the ring. To join, slip stitch.
3. Rounds two and onwards require two double crochets in each stitch. To join, slip stitch. Once the coaster is the size you want, keep adding rounds.

With crochet, you can entirely personalize the look and feel of your house to suit your tastes. The options range from useful goods like pillow coverings and table runners to beautiful ones like wall hangings.

# Stitching the Story's End

## Edging Techniques

### Classic Edgings: Fundamental Finishes

A crochet project's edgings are like the cherry on top; they give it that extra touch that elevates it from good to spectacular. The kind of edging you use will significantly alter the appearance and feel of your creation, from straightforward finishing to elaborate lace. We go into numerous edging styles and their corresponding guidelines below.

**Shell Edging: A series of double or triple crochets grouped together to create a scalloped edge**

Shell Edging gives every crocheted product a quirky, scalloped touch, making it a go-to for blankets, shawls, and even garments. Usually, it is constructed by stringing together double or triple crochets. This is how you do it:

1. One chain, turn.
2. In the first stitch, single crochet.
3. Make 5 double crochets in the following stitch after skipping one.
4. Skip the next stitch and single crochet.
5. Crosswise, repeat steps 3–4.

**Picot Edging: Small loops often added to other edging techniques, creating a decorative touch**

Picot Edging gives projects a delicate, ornamental finish and lends subtle appeal to edges. It looks fantastic, added to other stitches or used independently for a more minimalist look. How to make a picot is as follows:

1. After finishing a stitch, chain 3.
2. Creating a tiny loop, slip stitch into the first chain.
3. Continue using your usual stitching technique.

These picots can be included in elaborate lacework, single crochet borders, and shell edgings. It's a tiny thing, yet it has a significant effect!

**Single Crochet Border: A simple yet effective way to add a clean, finished look to a projec.**

You should always use a single crochet border to create a crisp, completed edge. Any project can look professional because of its extreme simplicity. This is how you do it:

1. If you're incorporating this into an ongoing project, join your yarn at any corner.
2. Chain 1 is first.

3. With three single crochets in each corner to keep it square, single crochet equally around the edge.
4. Join the first single crochet with a slip stitch.

It's a basic that works well for blankets, dishcloths, and almost anything that needs a tidy border.

**Texture & Dimension: Elevated Edging Techniques**

**Crab Stitch (Reverse Single Crochet): A unique stitch that offers a twisted, rope-like appearance**

Reverse single crochet, sometimes known as the crab stitch, creates a quirky, twisted edge that is both attractive and durable. How to apply this special touch is as follows:

1. With a slip stitch, begin at the corner of your object and attach your yarn there.
2. Chain 1.
3. Move your hook to the right and insert it into the stitch there instead of crocheting normally to the left.
4. Complete the stitch by yarning over, pulling through, then yarning over once more.
5. For every stitch, repeat this while going to the right.

For blankets, caps, or bags, it's a fantastic finish!

**Block Edging: A series of square or rectangular stitches, creating a blocky or stepped effect**

Block Edging gives your project a geometric finish and a pleasing appearance. Here is how to go about it:

1. With a slip stitch, join your yarn at the project's corner.
2. Single crochet in the first stitch after the chain.

3. Skip the next 3 stitches after chaining 3.

4. In the stitch after, single crochet.

5. Up until you reach the edge, repeat steps 4 and 5.

**Loop Stitch Border: An edging with a series of loops that can be left as-is or trimmed to create a fringe-like appearance**

Your project will have a fun, fringe-like feel thanks to the Loop Stitch Border. Making it entails the following:

1. Use a slip stitch to join your yarn to your project.

2. In the first stitch, yarn over, hook into the next stitch, and pull through.

3. Make a loop by extending the yarn by about an inch before finishing the single crochet.

4. To finish the single crochet and catch the loop, yarn over.

5. Follow steps 3-5 all the way around.

With its unique border, which adds texture, it looks excellent on blankets, scarves, and even clothing.

**Lacy & Openwork Edgings: Delicate Details**

**Fan Edging: A series of spaced-apart stitches creating fan-like structures for an airy finish**

Your projects will have a lovely, breezy touch thanks to fan edging. This is how to make it:

1. Use a slip stitch to connect yarn to the edge of your creation.

2. Chain three stitches to form the first double crochet.

3. Complete 4 additional double crochets in the same stitch.

4. Single crochet in the next stitch after skipping the next two.

5.  To create another fan, skip 2 more stitches and work 5 double crochets on the next stitch.
6.  Go around the edge and repeat steps 4-5.

Perfect for giving shawls, blankets, or clothing an elegant finish.

**Arch Stitch Edging: Producing a series of arches, which can be embellished with picots or other stitches**

.A border, or edging, gives your work a refined, airy feel. Creating it is as follows:

1.  Put yarn on the edge of your creation and slip stitch it.
2.  Your first double crochet will be a chain of three.
3.  Work 4 additional double crochets in the same stitch.
4.  Next, single crochet in the next stitch after skipping the next two.
5.  A second fan will be created by skipping the next two stitches and working five double crochets in the following stitch.
6.  All the way around, repeat steps 4-5.

Ideal for giving shawls, blankets, or clothing an elegant finishing touch.

**V-Stitch Border: An openwork border technique that gives a delicate and lacy effect to the project's edge**

Thanks to the V-Stitch Border, your crocheted objects will have a delicate and lacy finish.
How to Stitch a V-Stitch Border

1.  At the corner of your piece, slip-stitch the yarn together.
2.  To count as your first double crochet, chain 3.
3.  Crochet twice in the same location. Your first V-stitch is created by this.
4.  1 stitch is skipped.

5.  Work 1 double crochet, 1 chain, then 1 more double crochet in the following stitch. Another V-stitch, there.
6.  Steps 4-5 should be followed as you proceed.

Excellent for table runners, shawls, and blankets.

## Joining Pieces Together

**Seamless Joins: For Invisible Connections**

**Whip Stitch Join: Using a yarn needle to weave the pieces together, creating a nearly invisible seam**

A simple technique for attaching crochet pieces together seamlessly is the whip stitch join. This is how you do it:

1.  The incorrect sides of the parts you want to combine should be facing out.
2.  Matching yarn is threaded onto a knitting needle.
3.  The back loop of the first stitch on one piece and the back loop of the corresponding stitch on the other piece must both be passed through by the needle.
4.  With even tension, pull the yarn through.
5.  Stitch the back loops of each set of matching stitches as you go along.

This method works well for seams on clothing or afghans.

**Slip Stitch Join: Joining pieces with a crochet hook, creating a flat seam that blends with the rest of the work**

The slip stitch join is a sleek method of joining crochet pieces, which yields a flat seam that blends in perfectly with your work. This is how:

1.  Set the proper sides of the parts you are connecting up in order.
2.  Starting at the stitch you want to join first, thread your crochet hook through both layers of fabric.
3.  Pull through each loop on the hook with additional yarn.
4.  For each corresponding stitch across the sections, repeat steps 2-3.

**Single Crochet Join: Creates a raised ridge on the right side, adding a decorative touch or utilized on the wrong side for a flatter appearance**

The right side of your work will have a characteristic elevated ridge created by the single crochet join that can be used as decoration. Simply carry out this motion on the opposite side for a flatter appearance. What to do is as follows:

1.  Edge-to-edge aligns your components.
2.  The first stitch on both pieces should be entered with your hook.
3.  Pull through both loops on the hook after yarning over once more.
4.  Do this for each group of corresponding stitches.

**Lacy & Decorative Joins: Adding Flair to Your Connections**

**Join-As-You-Go: A technique especially popular for granny squares and lace motifs, where pieces are joined during the crochet process instead of afterward**

The join-as-you-go technique is a game-changer for projects like granny squares or lace motifs. You attach pieces as you crochet rather than sewing them together later. This is how:

1.  Till you reach a corner or the point of joining, begin crocheting one piece.
2.  Place your hook in the correct stitch on the portion you are attaching to.
3.  A slip stitch is used to assemble the parts.
4.  With the first piece, carry with your pattern by joining at each corner or indicated join point.

**Braided Join: Producing a beautiful, braided effect between pieces, adding both texture and a decorative touch**

The Braided Join technique adds texture and decoration to your product by braiding a striking seam between components. How to execute:

1.  Keep the incorrect sides of the two parts you want to link together.
2.  Start single crochet with a fresh strand of yarn from one edge and go through both layers.
3.  Complete the single crochet, but do not yarn over or pull through.
4.  Instead, place the hook into the subsequent stitch, then raise a loop.
5.  Pull through all of the loops on the hook after yarning over.
6.  Repeat steps 4 and 5 around the edge for a lovely, braided join.

**Scalloped Join: A series of arches or scallops that create a lacy, decorative seam between two pieces**

The scalloped join adds a fanciful, lacy seam, which is ideal for blankets or clothing that needs a decorative touch. This is how:

1.  Set the pieces you want to join in a line.
2.  Start with a slip stitch to link your yarn into one piece.
3.  Slip stitch into the following stitch after chaining five.
4.  Make a single crochet into the second piece's matching stitch.
5.  The method should be repeated to produce the chain-5 loops that make up your scallops.

Continue until the desired length of the scalloped join is reached!

**Advanced Joining Techniques: Beyond the Basics**

**Russian Join: A method to join two yarn ends without knots, using a yarn needle**

When joining two ends of yarn, the Russian Join is a game-changer for those who want to prevent knots. Here is a short instruction:

1. With one yarn's end, thread a yarn needle.
2. Make a loop by weaving the needle back through the yarn for about 2 inches.
3. Close the loop tightly, but leave a little circle behind.
4. With the second yarn end, repeat the procedure.
5. Place one loop inside the other, then tighten by pulling on both yarn ends.

This results in a secure, knot-free joint that is almost undetectable in the finished product.

**Flat Braid Join: Creates a beautiful, three-dimensional braid between motifs**

The Flat Braid Join adds depth and intricacy to your artwork by creating a gorgeous, 3D braided look between motifs. This is how you do it:

1. On your hook, tie a slipknot first.
2. Place your two themes side by side.
3. Start at one corner of both layers and thread your hook through.
4. Make a loop with yarn and draw it up.
5. Make a slip stitch by yarning back over and pulling through all the loops on the hook.
6. Chain three, omit the first stitch from each motif, then slip stitch through the following threads of both motifs.
7. Up until you reach the other corner, repeat from * to *.

**Interlocking Join: An intricate method that weaves the edges of two pieces together, creating a secure and decorative connection**

The Interlocking Join creates a strong yet beautiful seam by weaving the edges of two elements together. To perform:

1.  On your hook, tie a slipknot first.

2.  Hold the two pieces with the incorrect sides facing out.

3.  Your hook should be inserted into the first stitch on both pieces.

4.  Make a loop with yarn and draw it up.

5.  Reverse the yarn and draw it through both loops to complete one crochet.

6.  Hook into the subsequent stitch on the first piece, then the subsequent stitch on the second. Only one crochet.

7.  From * to *, repeat till the end.

This technique produces an interlocking, secure, aesthetically pleasing, and useful seam.

## Finishing Touch

**Perfecting the Border: The Frame to Your Masterpiece**

Making the border perfect is similar to framing your crocheted work. It adds structure and a polished finish. Start with a slip knot on your hook to create a straightforward single crochet border. Pull up a loop after inserting the hook into the first stitch and yarning over. Reverse the yarn and draw it through both hook loops. In every stitch around your object, repeat this step. Add two or three single crochets for a clean turn when working around corners. This gives your work a crisp, completed edge that enhances it.

**Importance of Borders: A discussion on how borders can give your project a complete, polished look, prevent edges from curling, and add structural integrity**

In crochet crafts, borders have several uses. They do two things: first, they give your work a finished, polished look that exclaims, "Hey, this project is finished and fabulous!" Second, a well-chosen border can keep your project's edges from curling, keeping it neat and level. Borders also add structural integrity. They become less likely to fray or stretch over time by strengthening the edges. The border should be the frame that highlights and protects your crocheted creation.

**Choosing the Right Border: Factors to consider, such as project type, yarn weight, and desired aesthetics**

The right border may make or break the entire project, much like choosing the ideal frame for a painting. First, think about the preparation. Is it a blanket, a piece of clothing, or a decorative object? Various projects necessitate various border types. Consider the yarn weight you used as well. A finer yarn may benefit from a more delicate border, whereas a chunkier yarn may look excellent with a basic, robust border. Finally, what mood are you trying to convey? Elegant, quirky, or traditional? Your whole project's aesthetic should be reflected in your border.

**Popular Border Techniques: Detailed walkthroughs of some beloved border styles, such as picot edges, lace trims, and ribbed borders, along with troubleshooting tips for achieving a flat, non-wavy edge**

An outstanding crochet project can be achieved by using common border techniques. Lace trimmings give garments a romantic atmosphere, while picot edges are ideal for a subtle ornamental accent. Ribbed borders can completely affect the game if you're trying for something more regimented. Though watch out for that dreadful wavy edge! Always count your stitches to prevent this, and you can do a gauge swatch for the border just like you would for the main item. Blocking the product may frequently eliminate waviness, ensuring your creation has the best finish possible.

**Block and Shape: Giving Form to Your Creations**

The unsung crochet heroes of blocking and shaping are crucial to giving your work a polished, finished appearance. To establish the shape of your finished piece, block it by wetting it and attaching it to a flat surface. This is especially important for tasks like stretching out elaborate motifs for lace shawls. Shaping, aon the other hand, involves molding your creation as you go; it's very important when making amigurumi and clothing.

Both lend shape and organization to your work, transforming a solid undertaking into a stunning masterpiece.

**Why Block?: An overview of how blocking sets stitches, evens out any inconsistencies, and gives a professional finish**

The magic wand of crochet, blocking rapidly transforms your work from amateur to expert level. It secures the stitches, resulting in a tidy, consistent appearance to your work. Do you have any minor errors or inconsistencies? By giving your stitches an instruction on how to behave, blocking helps even those out. In the end, it provides your product that polished, finished appearance that distinguishes it from the "good enough" from the "wow, you made that?" level. Anyone who is committed to their crocheting craft must complete this vital phase.

**Methods of Blocking: Exploring different techniques such as wet blocking, steam blocking, and spray blocking, along with the types of projects best suited for each**

There are several choices available to you for blocking! Natural textiles like wool work well with wet blocking, which involves soaking the garment before shaping it. Acrylics respond nicely to steam blocking, which is a little quicker. Hold a steam iron over your project without touching the yarn, please. For smaller, faster jobs, spray blocking is fantastic; just spritz and shape. Each technique has a best-case scenario of its own. For instance, lacework benefits greatly from wet blocking, whereas granny squares may only require a little steam. For the best results, select your method based on the requirements of your project.

**Tools and Tips: A guide to using blocking boards, pins, and wires effectively, along with advice on maintaining the shape and structure of your finished item**

Have you completed and are ready to block your crocheted item? Great! Let's now discuss some tools and advice. For attaining those straight lines and ideal shapes, blocking boards are essential. The best pins to use for securing everything in place are rust-proof ones. Blocking wires can significantly alter the outcome for more elaborate designs like circles or fine lace. An advice? To maintain uniform spacing, use a ruler or measuring tape. Once your creation has been blocked and dried, coil it up or store it flat to preserve the stylish appearance of the hard-earned shape.

**Embellishments: Adding Personality and Flair**

Ah, decorations! They serve as the finishing touch for your crocheted projects. Beads, buttons, ribbons, or even wacky yarn in a contrasting color are acceptable embellishments. Consider making a basic beanie. Add a pompom or a charming appliqué, and presto! You have a one-of-a-kind item! These minor details give the work your stamp and transform it from "that's nice" to "OMG, where'd you get that?" So don't be afraid to add some texture or a little glitter. Making it your own is the key.

**The Role of Embellishments: Discussion on how additions like beads, tassels, buttons, and appliqués can transform a simple project into something unique**

Sincerely, embellishments affect the game. Consider them the "seasoning" that makes a dish better. Beads, tassels, buttons, and appliqués offer a special touch to crochet designs. Got a simple scarf? It becomes a convertible infinity loop when a few buttons are stitched on. Basic blanket? It can seem boho-chic if a row of tassels is on edge. These tiny touches give a project your unique touch and transform it from nice into "wow, that's amazing!" So feel free to adorn your stitches!

**Techniques for Adding Beads: Exploring pre-stringing versus the crochet hook method for beadwork**

Oh, crochet with beads? Heavenly compatibility! Pre-stringing and the crochet hook method are the primary techniques for incorporating those sparkling gems into your yarn creation. To pre-string, you must first thread all your beads onto the yarn. It works well when you are certain of each bead's placement. The crochet hook method, on the other hand, enables you to include beads as you go. Simply pull a bead onto a thread with the hook—incredibly practical for more freestyle creations. Choose based on the requirements of your project because each method has benefits!

**Creating Tassels, Fringes, and Pom-Poms: Step-by-step guides for making consistent, lush additions to projects. Tips on placement and attachment for durability and aesthetic appeal**

Fringes, pom-poms, and tassels? Please, yes! They serve as the icing on a crochet sundae. Simply wrap yarn around a piece of cardboard, snip one end, and tie off the top to create tassels. Cut even strands of yarn and use a crochet hook to join them to create fringes. Pom-poms are a lot of fun to make; you only need to wound the yarn around a pom-pom maker or your hand, tie it tightly in the middle, and clip the loops. But hey, the position is everything! For style and longevity, firmly attach these treats, usually in the corners or edges.

# Conclusion

It is easy to feel as though you are traveling through a labyrinth when attempting to navigate the vast world of crochet, which is loaded with infinite stitches, patterns, and possibilities. With the book "Stitch by Stitch: An Essential Guide to Creative Crocheting," our goal was to provide you with the resources, information, and ideas you require to make this journey not only manageable but also profoundly satisfying.

In the section titled "The Supply Spectrum," we went over the specifics of crochet's main elements and led you through an in-depth review of the many required supplies. Understanding your materials is essential to the practice of any craft, and crochet is no exception to this rule. This topic is covered in "What You'll Need," so check it out. The articles "All About Yarn" and "Yarn Weight Guidelines" dove deeper into the qualities, textures, and characteristics of many types of yarn, which assisted you in making more educated decisions regarding the materials to use for your projects.

The book "Crochet Cornerstones" dispelled some obscurity surrounding crochet lingo by introducing fundamental concepts. The book "The Crocheter's Dictionary" included an alphabetical list of crochet words and abbreviations, while the book "A Guide to Pattern Reading" was written to make the process of reading crochet patterns less scary and more akin to the fun of solving a puzzle.

The book "Stitch Mastery" included a variety of techniques and procedures, beginning with fundamental stitches that served as the building blocks in the chapter "Classic Crochet Stitches" and progressing to more complicated methods in the chapter "Advanced Stitches." The section titled "Techniques for Shaping and Joining" discussed how to construct various forms and shapes, giving your work a three-dimensional quality. In the section titled "Colorwork and Patterns in Crochet," we discussed the aesthetic value of color, and in the section titled "Special Techniques," we moved one step further into unorthodox ways.

The section of the book titled "Blueprints in Yarn" was the most instructive and provided you with tasks you could do, such as baby booties and granny square blankets. Each project was intended to provide both learning and creating opportunities, preparing you for the subsequent challenge and providing you with a finished product you might be pleased with.

However, a voyage is only finished once it has a conclusion or a proper finish in the crochet language. In the concluding portions, the emphasis was placed on this significant point. You learned how to give your projects a finished, expert appearance by taking the "Edging Techniques" course. You discovered that the correct edge may take your work from excellent to knockout, and you used techniques ranging from straightforward single crochet borders to intricate lace trimmings. The tutorial titled "Joining Pieces Together" walked you through the many techniques that may be used to combine individual crochet components into one cohesive whole. This was expanded in the book "Finishing Touch" to cover the unique finishing touches that can give your product a distinctively personal quality, such as beads, tassels, or even a strategically placed button.

As we approach this book's final chapter, you must take some time to think about the transformative potential of this age-old craft. Your crochet vocabulary grows with every hook and skein of yarn you acquire, as well as each design you decipher and every stitch you perfect. Remember that the real magic resides not just in the final product but in the process of getting there — stitch by complex stitch — whether you crochet to relax, present, sell, or simply for the joy of making something new. If you crochet for any of these reasons or simply for the fun of creating something new, remember that the real magic lies in the finished result.

Although we covered many subjects, the crochet world is much more expansive. Beyond the pages of this book, there are diverse crochet techniques, vintage designs updated for the present, and an expanding online community of crochet lovers like you. You can share your works and learn from others using the unlimited resources and inspiration that social media platforms, blogs, and YouTube channels provide.

Take notice of the influence of your neighborhood, too. Groups and workshops focusing on crocheting are excellent sources for practical instruction and interpersonal contact. The knowledge of more seasoned craftsmen can frequently help you navigate difficulties that printed instructions sometimes need to be more clearly explained. Crocheting is a flexible activity that suits all personalities, whether you're a lone wolf who appreciates the meditative seclusion of crocheting in a quiet corner or a social butterfly who flourishes in a group environment.

Making something by hand is a bold act of mindfulness and sustainability in a world of quick fashion and disposable commodities. Your handmade creations have value beyond their monetary value since they are infused with love, care, and time. So keep in mind that the overall worth of your work is much bigger than the total number of stitches, whether you're crocheting a gift for a special someone or making something to sell.

The versatility of crochet is ultimately what makes it beautiful. Yarn is your medium, and you are the artist. Every project offers the chance to try something new, make mistakes and learn from them, hone your talents, and, most importantly, express yourself. The route to mastery is a twisting one with many fascinating deviations rather than a straight one. Accept them because each turn in the road tells a story, each error teaches a lesson, and each project is a new chapter in your crochet saga's ongoing journey.

So, as you lay this book down and take up your crochet hook, remember that you are also stitch by stitch, creating your own path, not just making things. The sky is the limit no matter where this creative road leads you. Dream boldly, stitch bravely, and never stop discovering everything crochet offers.

We are grateful that you have chosen to take "Stitch by Stitch" along on your journey of creative expression. We have high hopes that reading and following along with it has been as rewarding for you as it has been for us to develop. In the voyage, may you discover many more stitches, designs, and lovely things to crochet.

Have fun with your crocheting!

# BONUS: YOUTUBE PLAYLIST

Before You Learn to Crochet

50 Crochet Tools For Beginners: EVERYTHING You Need To Crochet!!

The Crocheter's Guide to All Things Yarn for Beginners

How to Slip Knot and Chain - Crochet Lesson 1

CROCHET 101 | Basic Stitches for Absolute Beginners

Common Crochet Mistakes and Beginner Frustrations

25+ CROCHET HACKS FOR BEGINNERS [Pro-Tips from a Crocheter with 20 Years Experience]